GREAT GIFTS™
WRAP IT UP

Library of Congress Cataloging-in-Publication Data Wrap it up. p. cm. — Includes index. ISBN 0-86573-986-2 — 1. Gift
wrapping. 2. Paper work. 3. Box craft. 4. Ornamental boxes. I. Cy DeCosse Incorporated. TT870.W73 1996
745.54 — dc20 96-10564 CIP

Table of **Contents**

SPRAY-PAINTED
Wrapping papers

A can of spray paint and sheets of brown or white craft paper are all you need to create handmade wrapping paper.

Place inexpensive flat objects on the paper and spray over them to create decorative designs with little effort. Simple paper doilies produce unique and original patterns that are a cross between a romantic Victorian style and 1970s tie-dye.

To achieve a clean, contemporary look or a casual, country look, use removable tape to make a checked or geometric design on paper before applying paint. This style is fresh and uncluttered and is very easy to create.

For an informal yet unique look, crumple paper and apply paint by spraying it at an angle from one side. The paint will color the areas of the paper facing you, leaving the hidden areas unpainted. This technique creates a textured look both with the physical crumpling of the paper and the uneven painting. Experimentation helps, so try this technique on newspaper first until you achieve the desired result.

Doily Design

MATERIALS

❖Sheets of brown or white craft paper
❖Paper doilies ❖Aerosol adhesive ❖Aerosol acrylic paint in desired color

☞ Doilies can be reused on other portions of paper or on another sheet of paper after paint has dried.

☞ For less defined edges around doilies, omit spray adhesive. This will produce slight clouding around edges of the doilies.

☞ Add a shimmering effect to flat paint colors by spraying metallic paint lightly over first color before removing doilies.

1 Spray a light coat of adhesive on the back sides of doilies. Gently press doilies adhesive-side-down onto craft paper, arranging them as desired.

2 Spray a few light coats of paint over surface of doilies to the depth of color you desire. When paint is dry, remove doilies. ▼

1 Crumple paper by gathering it up in your fists. Slightly flatten it on top of work surface.

2 Spray paper from a low angle from one side. When paper is dry, flatten it for use.

Crumpled Design

MATERIALS

❖Sheets of brown or white craft paper
❖Aerosol acrylic paint in desired color

---

1 Apply removable tape to paper in a lattice design, pressing it down slightly. Spray a few light layers of paint over taped paper to the depth of color you desire. When paint is dry, remove tape.

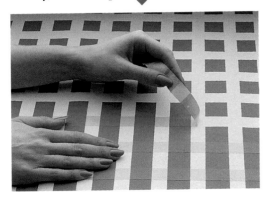

☞ *Choose a durable paper that will not tear when tape is removed.*

Checked Design

MATERIALS

❖Sheets of brown or white craft paper
❖Removable tape ❖Aerosol acrylic paint in desired color

☞ *Randomly placed pieces of tape will produce a spontaneous pattern with less effort.*

STAMPED
Gift wraps
& Cards

Turn plain paper or bags into one-of-a-kind gift wraps, using rubber stamps. Stamps can also be used on ribbons, tissue paper, greeting cards, or gift tags. Purchase any of dozens of premade stamps, which are available in art supply stores, stationery shops, or gift stores. Or create a truly personal touch with your own stamps, made by cutting designs into artist's erasers or printing blocks, using a mat knife. For easier cutting, select designs with simple details.

Handmade Stamps

MATERIALS

❖Soft artist's eraser or printing block
❖Tracing paper ❖Transfer paper ❖Mat
knife ❖Stamp pad ❖Plain wrapping
paper, tissue paper, paper
bags, blank greeting
cards, or ribbon

☞ *Stamp pads are available at art supply stores and print shops.*

☞ *Some metallic inks may leave oil marks on fabric ribbons. For best results with fabric ribbons, apply a heavy amount of spray starch to them; then press them with an iron before stamping the designs.*

1 Trace desired design onto tracing paper. Using transfer paper, transfer design to smooth side of artist's eraser or printing block. Cut about ⅛" (3 mm) deep into eraser along design lines, using mat knife.

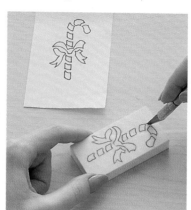

2 Remove large background area around design by cutting horizontally through the edge of eraser and up to the cuts made at the design outline.

3 Cut and remove the narrow spaces within the design by cutting at an angle along each edge; remove the small background areas.

4 Press the stamp firmly onto the stamp pad; lift and repeat as necessary until the design on the stamp is evenly coated with ink. Press stamp straight down onto desired surface, using even pressure.

Doodle designs

Give your gifts a whimsical and childlike look by doodling your own designs on wrapping paper and cards. You don't need to be an artist or even have very good handwriting to create fun and festive designs. Doodle holiday designs, stick figures, phrases, the recipient's name—anything you like.

The easiest way to create the right look for wrapping paper is through repetition. Practice your design first on scrap paper, then repeat it frequently on plain or colored craft paper. This will give your paper a patterned look. If you are right-handed, begin your pattern on the left side of the paper, or start on the right side if you are left-handed, to prevent smudging your work.

Purchase plain greeting cards from stationery stores and embellish them with your own doodle designs. When writing, misspell words or invert a few letters to build on the childlike look.

Use colored markers, crayons, or even metallic markers to doodle your designs. Test markers on scrap paper first, since some will bleed through porous papers. Pencils are not recommended, since their markings will smudge when touched.

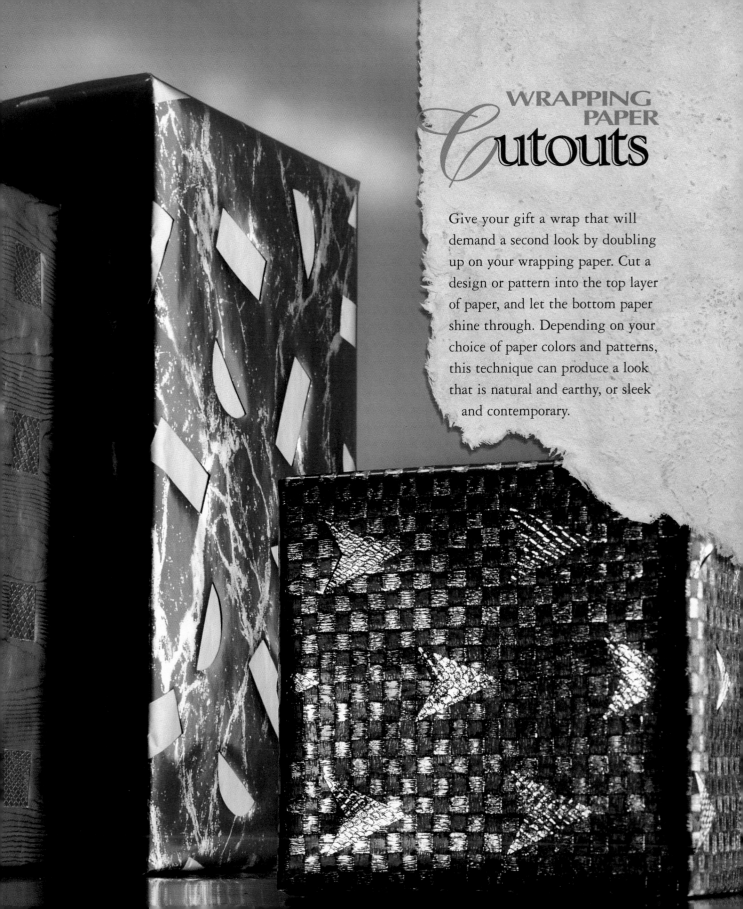

WRAPPING PAPER Cutouts

Give your gift a wrap that will demand a second look by doubling up on your wrapping paper. Cut a design or pattern into the top layer of paper, and let the bottom paper shine through. Depending on your choice of paper colors and patterns, this technique can produce a look that is natural and earthy, or sleek and contemporary.

Window Cutouts

MATERIALS

❖Two coordinating wrapping papers
❖Light-colored felt-tip pen ❖Cork-backed metal ruler ❖Mat knife and cutting surface ❖Newspaper
❖Aerosol adhesive

1 Cut both wrapping papers a little larger than needed to wrap your gift. Set paper for bottom layer aside.

2 Mark 1" (2.5 cm) squares on the back of the paper for top layer, using a cork-backed metal ruler as a guide; space them every 2" (5 cm). Use a felt-tip pen to draw lines; don't press too hard, or impressions of the lines will show through the front of the paper. (Dark pen was used to show detail). ▼

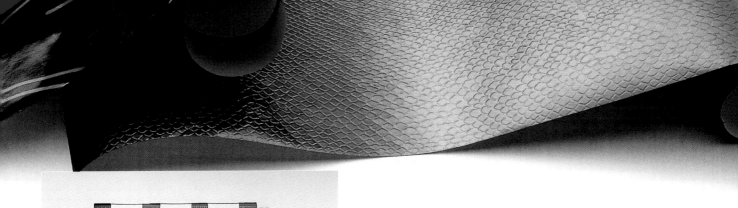

4 Place cut paper facedown on newspaper. Spray with aerosol adhesive. Place paper for bottom layer facedown over adhesive so it shows through cutouts; carefully smooth out any air bubbles. Allow to dry about 15 minutes. ▼

3 Place marked paper facedown on cutting surface; cut out squares, using mat knife.

5 Trim edges of layered paper to fit gift box, and wrap box.

☞ *For a random, casual look, use a mat knife to cut freehand designs into paper.*

☞ *If desired, omit the aerosol adhesive and simply double-wrap the box with the cutout paper on top.*

☞ *Keep patterns and designs of cutouts small, so paper folds easily around package.*

☞ *Create dramatic color contrasts or subtle plays on color in your selection of wrapping papers. Shades of the same color can have a soft effect. Hot pink glowing through purple, on the other hand, is a real eye-catcher.*

Plastic wrap
PRESENTATIONS

Plastic wrap, available in a variety of colors, is an inexpensive and versatile product for creative wrapping ideas. It can be used to decoratively protect trays of food items or loaves of bread. You can make colorful bows and line boxes or bags with it. Or use it to individually wrap cupcakes or party favors.

For especially festive wrapping paper, sprinkle confetti over tissue paper, cover it with colored wrap, and seal the edges with transparent tape.

Wrapped Bread

MATERIALS

❖Bread ❖Colored plastic wrap

🎁

☞ *If desired, add plastic-wrap bow, shown below, to wrapped loaf.*

1 Cut a sheet of colored plastic wrap five times as long as loaf of bread. Place loaf lengthwise in center of plastic wrap.

2 Position a second sheet of plastic, long enough to cover bread, over the top of the loaf, pressing sheet to loaf. Bring short sides of bottom sheet up, and press onto top sheet.

3 Pull opposite ends of bottom sheet over top of loaf; twist to seal. Fluff ends to form a bow; trim ends, if desired.

Plastic-wrap Bow

MATERIALS

❖One or more shades of colored plastic wrap

🎁

1 Cut a sheet, 12" (30.5 cm) square, of plastic wrap. Fold two opposite sides toward each other to meet at center. Gather and pinch wrap along center line. Set aside.

2 Repeat twice more with the same color or another color of wrap. Stack bows; tie at center with twisted strip of plastic wrap. Twist and fan ends of bow for desired appearance.

1 Cut sheet, 6" (15 cm) square, of plastic wrap. Place thumb in center of sheet; mold wrap around thumb to form nest. Repeat for desired number of nests.

2 Place chocolates in nests; arrange filled nests in gift box.

MATERIALS

❖One or more shades of colored plastic wrap ❖Assorted chocolate candies or bon-bons ❖Gift box

1 Place pink sheet of plastic wrap over yellow sheet so the edges match. Position carrot diagonally across center of layered wraps. Fold corner of wrap up 2" (5 cm) to meet the pointed end of carrot.

2 Bring one corner of wrap over carrot toward opposite corner; press flat to seal. Roll the carrot in plastic wrap toward overlapped corners. Remove carrot, being careful to keep the shape of the wrap. Fill the shaped wrap with candies, nuts, or raisins; twist top to seal.

Carrot package Favors

MATERIALS

❖One sheet each, 12" (30.5 cm) square, of pink and yellow plastic wraps ❖Small candies, nuts, or raisins ❖One sheet, 6" (15 cm) square, green plastic wrap ❖7" (18 cm) washed carrot

Plastic wrap projects courtesy of Reynolds® Crystal Color® Plastic Wrap.

3 Fold green sheet of plastic wrap in half. Wind the folded edge around the top of "carrot"; secure with twisted strip of yellow wrap. Use carrots in place of bows on gift boxes.

UNIQUE *Wrapping* papers

Almost anything made of paper can be used to wrap gifts. Look for vintage magazines, foreign newspapers, and other interesting papers that can be used as wrap. These items provide interesting alternatives to the typical glossy, printed wrapping paper.

Try some of the following materials as gift wrap:

- Maps
- Empty paper flour bags
- Smoothed-out paper twist
- Advertisements cut from vintage magazines
- Aluminum foil
- Foreign newspapers
- Posters
- Calendar pages
- Photocopied menus or personal photographs
- Poems or sheet music

To give photocopied items an aged appearance, tea-dye them. Brew strong tea, about four tea bags per 1 quart (1 L) of water; leave bags in water, and dip paper in water until desired appearance is achieved. Remove paper from tea, and spread on flat surface covered with paper towels to dry.

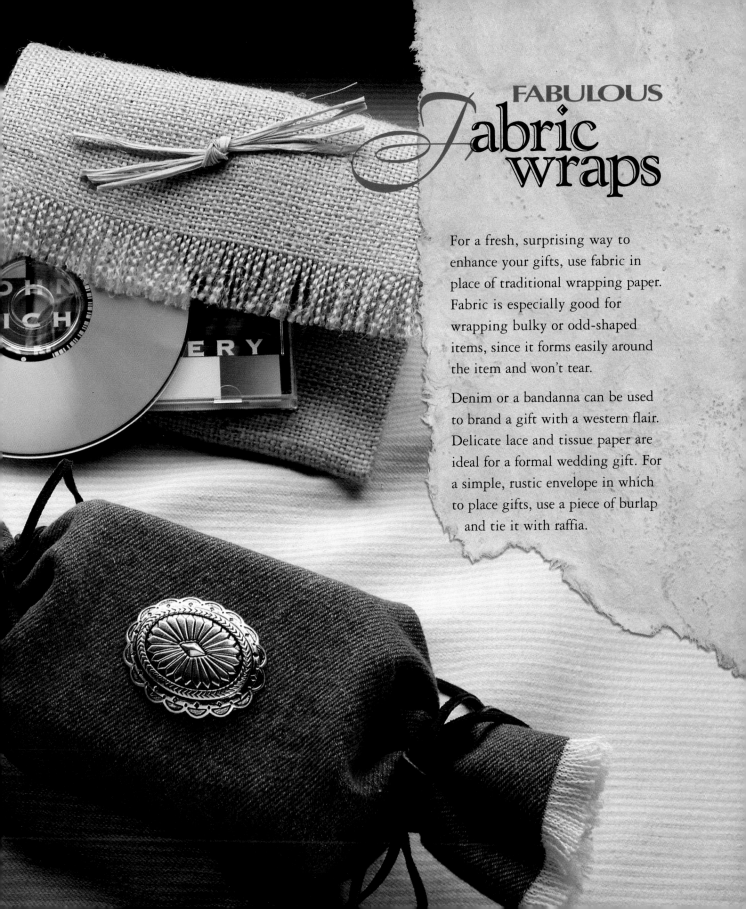

FABULOUS
Fabric wraps

For a fresh, surprising way to enhance your gifts, use fabric in place of traditional wrapping paper. Fabric is especially good for wrapping bulky or odd-shaped items, since it forms easily around the item and won't tear.

Denim or a bandanna can be used to brand a gift with a western flair. Delicate lace and tissue paper are ideal for a formal wedding gift. For a simple, rustic envelope in which to place gifts, use a piece of burlap and tie it with raffia.

Western Roll

MATERIALS

❖Denim fabric ❖Leather lacing or ribbon
❖Hot glue gun and glue sticks ❖Western-
style metal charm or button

1 Cut a piece of denim that is wide enough to fit around your gift and has several inches of extra fabric on sides. Fray sides slightly by pulling several rows of threads out.

2 Roll fabric around gift with frayed sides on left and right. Gather sides together and tie with leather lacing or ribbon. Fluff gathered sides to open them. (There is no need to secure raw edge on underside of the package.)

3 Secure a metal charm or button to top of package, using hot glue.

☞ *A bandanna also works well for this style of wrap, and if no charm is attached, the bandanna becomes an additional gift.*

☞ *Create other looks by using different types of fabric and ribbon. Fabric with a colorful cartoon print and colored shoelaces or barrettes for ties can be used for a child's gift.*

Lace Pouch

MATERIALS

❖Lace fabric ❖Tissue paper ❖Ribbons

1 Cut one piece of lace fabric large enough to be gathered around your gift at the top. Place layers of tissue paper over lace fabric at 45° angles. This will add body to your package.

1 Cut piece of burlap long enough to wrap around the gift one-and-a-half times; allow an extra 2" (5 cm) in width for the seams plus twice the thickness of gift.

2 Fray top end of burlap by removing several rows of threads, as shown opposite.

Burlap Envelope

MATERIALS

❖Burlap fabric ❖Hot glue gun and glue sticks ❖Raffia ❖Large-eyed needle

3 Fold in ½" (1.3 cm) on long sides of fabric; secure with hot glue. Fold in ½" (1.3 cm) on bottom edge; secure with hot glue. Fold bottom end of burlap over to within one-third of the length of the fabric. Secure sides with hot glue to create an envelope.

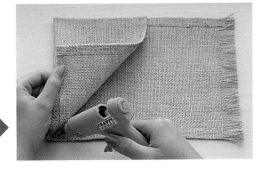

4 Thread raffia through back side of top flap, using a large-eyed needle; tie in a knot on the front side. Place the gift in the envelope and close flap.

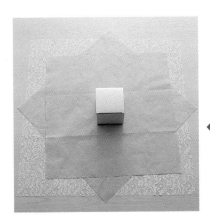

2 Place the gift in center of the tissue. Gather tissue at top of gift; secure with ribbon. Gather the lace at the top of the gift; tie with second ribbon.

☞ *Use one or more colors of tissue paper. For a wedding gift, use colors that correspond to the colors selected for the wedding. Baby shower gifts could be blue and pink.*

3 Embellish gift with additional ribbons, if desired. Trim edges of lace and ends of ribbon as desired.

Season's
Greetings

Natural cards
& WRAPS

Decorating your packages and
cards with natural embellishments
gives them a fresh, rustic look.
This style of wrapping is perfect
for handmade gifts like needlepoint
samplers or home-canned foods
from your garden.

Dried flowers, leaves, and
chilies, and preserved items like
juniper or mistletoe make ideal
embellishments for a naturally
wrapped gift. Handmade or
recycled papers and sisal rope
can also be used for accents.
You can use these items, found in
craft, floral, or stationery stores,
to accent cards, small
pine bandboxes, or plain
wrapped boxes.

Holiday Card

MATERIALS

❖Blank cards ❖Narrow gold cording or ribbon ❖Preserved juniper or mistletoe sprig ❖Gold-ink pen

1 Cut two small slits about ⅛" (3 cm) apart in a top corner of card. Thread gold cording through the slits. ▼

2 Place end of juniper sprig between the slits. Tie cording around the juniper. Write holiday greeting on front or inside of card with gold-ink pen.

☞ *Use this technique with a sprig of dried flowers suited to any season.*

Bay-leaf Bandbox

MATERIALS

❖Small, round pine bandbox ❖Rustic-looking art paper ❖Hot glue gun and glue sticks ❖Fresh bay leaves ❖Assorted dried flowers

1 Place lid of bandbox on paper; trace around the outer edge. Cut on marked line.

1 Wrap gift box with brown paper. Embellish box as desired with dried naturals; secure with hot glue.

2 Cut sisal rope long enough to reach diagonally across box with extra to create a handle. Slightly fray ends of rope. Using hot glue, secure one end of rope to top of box at corner. Twist rope over box to opposite corner, pushing it up to form a handle; secure end with hot glue.

Natural-wrapped Box

MATERIALS

❖Brown wrapping paper ❖Assorted dried naturals ❖Hot glue gun and glue sticks
❖Sisal rope

☞ *For a functional handle, use this style of wrapping for lightweight gifts.*

2 Crumple paper slightly. Gently flatten paper; secure to lid, using hot glue.

3 Attach a circle of bay leaves around edge of the lid, using hot glue; overlap leaves slightly. Accent lid with assorted dried flowers, using hot glue.

Bow making

Making big, beautiful bows for your gifts is easy. Craft ribbon is available in a wide variety of fabrics, and if you use a generous amount, you will end up with a truly luxurious bow. Use satin or gold wired ribbon for a formal and elegant look. Paper twist or checked gingham gives your package a rustic or homespun appearance. Instructions for making both traditional and cluster bows are given on the following pages.

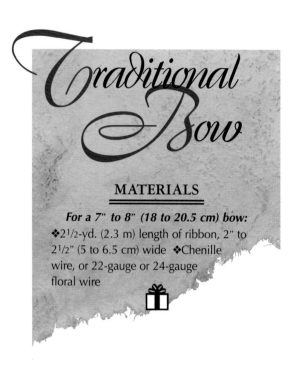

Traditional Bow

MATERIALS

For a 7" to 8" (18 to 20.5 cm) bow:
❖ 2½-yd. (2.3 m) length of ribbon, 2" to 2½" (5 to 6.5 cm) wide ❖ Chenille wire, or 22-gauge or 24-gauge floral wire

1 Cut 18" (46 cm) length from ribbon; set aside. Starting 8" to 12" (20.5 to 30.5 cm) from end of remaining ribbon, fold 3½" to 4" (9 to 10 cm) loop, with right side of ribbon facing out.

2 Fold a loop toward the opposite side, bringing ribbon under the tail to keep the right side of the ribbon facing out.

3 Continue making loops that fan slightly, until there are three or four loops on each side, with a second tail extending.

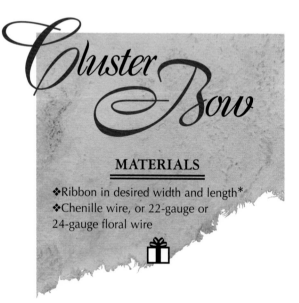

Cluster Bow

MATERIALS

❖ Ribbon in desired width and length*
❖ Chenille wire, or 22-gauge or 24-gauge floral wire

1 Place thumb and index finger at determined length for tail, with ribbon right side up. Fold ribbon back on itself at a diagonal, with wrong sides together, so ribbon forms a right angle.

2 Wrap ribbon over thumb to form center loop; secure with fingers. Twist ribbon one-half turn at underside of loop, so the right side of ribbon faces up. ▼

To estimate ribbon yardage, multiply the desired diameter of the bow by the desired number of loops. Add 6" (15 cm) for the center loop plus the desired length for tails and extra streamers, if desired.

4 Bend chenille wire around ribbon at center, twisting wire tightly and gathering ribbon. Hold wire firmly at the top, and turn the bow, twisting the wire snug.

5 Fold width of 18" (46 cm) length of ribbon into thirds through the middle portion of the ribbon. Tie this portion around the center of bow, knotting it on the back of the bow. Separate and fluff loops. Trim tails as desired.

3 Form first loop. Twist ribbon one-half turn, and form a loop on the opposite side.

4 Continue forming loops under the previous ones, alternating sides and twisting the ribbon so the right side always faces up; make each successive loop slightly larger than the loop above it.

5 Insert chenille wire through center of bow, when the final loop has been formed. Bend wire around ribbon at center, twisting wire tightly and gathering ribbon. Hold wire firmly at the top, and turn the bow, twisting the wire snug. Separate and fluff loops. Trim tails as desired.

Stiffened fabric
EMBELLISHMENTS

Fabric stiffener is easy to use and gives texture and character to fabric. Use the stiffened fabric to embellish cards, gift tags, or package tops. Create one-of-a-kind miniature collages, greeting cards, or bows that will be saved and remembered.

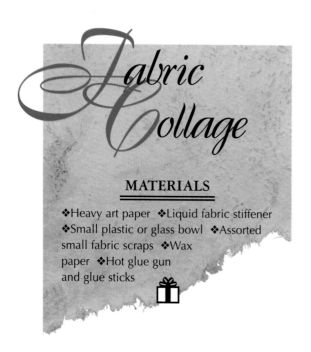

Fabric Collage

MATERIALS

❖Heavy art paper ❖Liquid fabric stiffener
❖Small plastic or glass bowl ❖Assorted
small fabric scraps ❖Wax
paper ❖Hot glue gun
and glue sticks

1 Determine the space available for the collage, whether it is going to be attached to a card or used in place of a bow on a gift box. Tear piece of art paper to fit the available space.

2 Pour the fabric stiffener into bowl. Dip small pieces of fabric scraps into the stiffener, making sure the scraps are saturated. Remove scraps from stiffener; set aside on sheet of wax paper.

Fan Card

MATERIALS

❖Large, plain greeting card made of heavy paper ❖Large pieces of scrap fabric
❖Liquid fabric stiffener ❖Small plastic or glass bowl ❖Wax paper ❖Plastic clothespin ❖Hot glue gun and glue sticks, or craft glue ❖Raffia or narrow ribbon

1 Cut a strip of fabric 1" (2.5 cm) wide and 4" (10 cm) longer than folded edge of card. Set aside. Cut an 11" × 2½" (28 × 6.5 cm) strip from second piece of fabric.

2 Pour fabric stiffener into bowl. Dip fabric strips into stiffener, making sure fabric is saturated. Remove pieces from stiffener; place on sheet of wax paper.

3 Arrange wet fabric scraps, one at a time, on piece of torn art paper. Overlap and bunch scraps to add texture. Allow to dry 2 to 3 hours.

4 Attach the dried collage to desired surface, using hot glue.

☞ *Framed Greeting Cards (page 48) lend themselves well to this type of treatment.*

☞ *Wash hands before arranging dipped fabric scraps on art paper.*

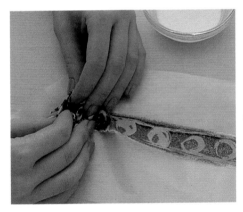

3 Crumple long, narrow strip of fabric along its length by gathering it slightly on a clean sheet of wax paper. Curve strip slightly. Allow to dry 2 to 3 hours.

4 Fold wider strip of fabric in an accordion fold, starting from its short side. Pinch one folded end together and secure with plastic clothespin; fan out fabric. Allow to dry 2 to 3 hours. Tie the pinched end with raffia.

5 Secure fan and crumpled strip on card, using hot glue. Trim ends of strip to match edges of card. Tie raffia around card along fold.

Stiffened fabric Bow

MATERIALS

❖Liquid fabric stiffener ❖Large plastic or glass bowl ❖45" (115 cm) length of cotton fabric ribbon, 2" to 2¹/₂" (5 to 7.5 cm) wide ❖Wax paper ❖Plastic clothespin ❖Hot glue gun and glue sticks

1 Pour fabric stiffener into bowl. Dip entire ribbon into stiffener, making sure ribbon is completely saturated; squeeze out excess stiffener. Lay ribbon facedown on long sheet of wax paper.

2 Fold right half of the ribbon over top toward center, creating a large loop and draping end of the ribbon in front of the loop. Stuff loop loosely with crushed wax paper so it holds its shape. Repeat with left half of ribbon.

☞ *This project makes a large bow. Use a shorter length of narrower ribbon and make smaller loops for a smaller bow.*

3 Pick up left end of the ribbon and create a second loop, starting at the base of the first loop and doubling back. Stuff second loop with crushed wax paper. Repeat with right side.

4 Cross ends of the ribbon in front of the loops. Gather and pinch center of bow, and fasten with plastic clothespin. Refine loops and ends of the ribbon to desired look while still wet. Allow to dry 2 to 3 hours.

5 Remove crushed wax paper from dry bow. Trim ends of ribbon, if desired. Secure bow to gift, using hot glue.

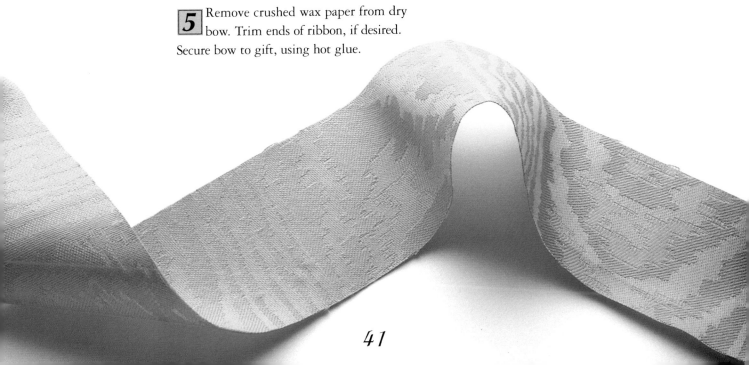

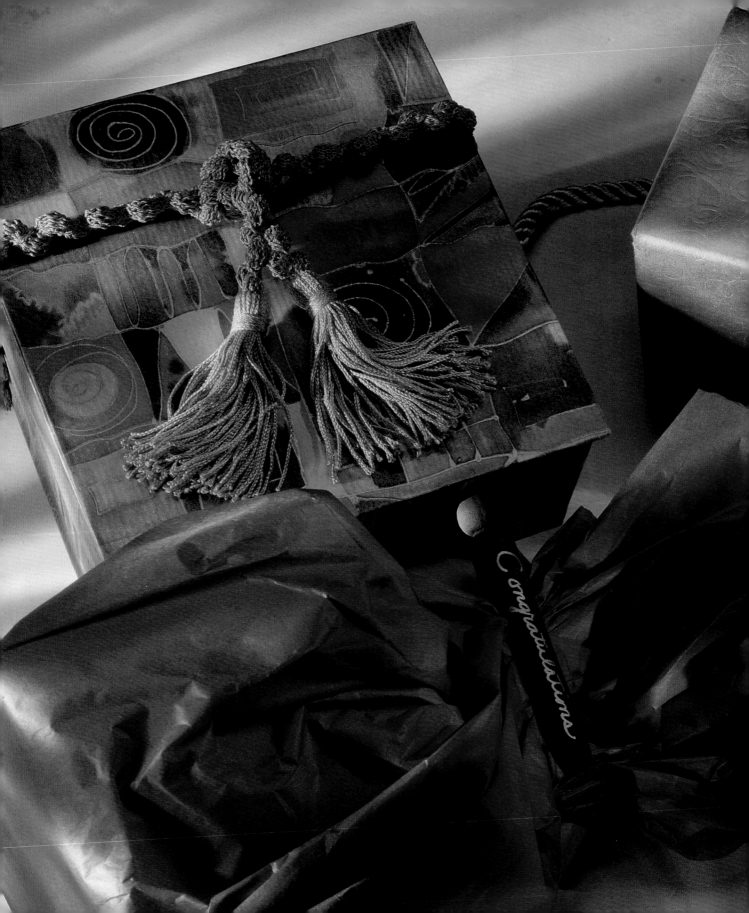

Package
EMBELLISHMENTS

Finding ways to accent your packages uniquely is as simple as looking around your house or a craft store. Look for costume jewelry, buttons, or pins at garage sales, auctions, and flea markets. Consider using scraps of cording, lace, or ribbon left over from sewing projects. Almost anything can be used to top a gift, even a package of seeds or a baby rattle.

Create ivy ribbons from silk ivy plants to give a light, summery look to your gifts. For a formal look, spray paint the ivy leaves gold or silver. Give a rich, sophisticated look to your package by wrapping it in elegant wrapping paper and accenting it with imitation pearls and rhinestones.

Cording can make an elegant and extremely easy package tie. Use cording with tassels on the ends, and simply tie it around the box with a bulky knot. Tie more than one color of cord around a box, or twist cords together before tying them.

Even something as simple as a clothespin can be turned into a package tie. Write your message on the side of a clothespin with a permanent-ink marker. Add a design with colored pens, or color the end with paint or a colored marker. Use the clothespin to secure gathered paper at the top of your package.

1 Remove leaves from silk ivy plant by peeling them from their plastic-and-wire backing.

Leaf Ribbon

MATERIALS

❖Silk ivy plant ❖Hot glue gun and glue sticks

2 Secure tip of an ivy leaf to base of a second leaf, using hot glue. Continue gluing leaf tips to bases until you have a chain long enough to fit around package plus 1" (2.5 cm) for overlap.

3 Wrap completed ivy ribbon around package; overlap ends at top of package, and secure with hot glue. If ribbon is not glued to the package, it can be reused. Glue additional leaves to center of ivy ribbon to create a "bow."

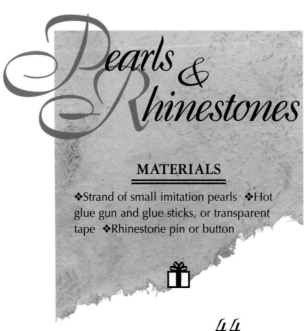

Pearls & Rhinestones

MATERIALS

❖Strand of small imitation pearls ❖Hot glue gun and glue sticks, or transparent tape ❖Rhinestone pin or button

1 Wind strand of pearls several times around wrapped package, wrapping ends to underside of box.

Cording Tie

☞ *Cording frays when cut. Take advantage of this by tying knots 1″ to 2″ (2.5 to 5 cm) from cut ends and then fraying ends up to knots to create a tasseled look. Or use cording with premade tassels on the ends.*

☞ *For an unfrayed look, apply liquid fray preventer to cording at location of desired cut. Allow to dry; then cut cording.*

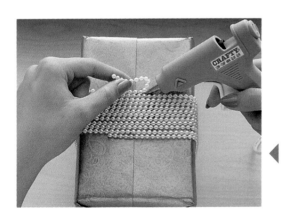

2 Glue ends of pearl strand to underside of box, or secure in place with transparent tape. If desired, place small drops of hot glue between strands so they stay in place.

3 Use hot glue to secure rhinestone pin or button to top of box in center of pearl strands.

UNIQUE Gift tags & CARDS

In addition to bows and ribbons, you may want to add a special gift tag or card to your package. Add a personal touch by making your own cards or gift tags.

Tin tags are a great way to dress up your gift presentation and recycle at the same time. Look at the bottoms of foil pie plates or cake pans. You will usually find an embossed design on them. Cut out the design for a simple tag that needs only a little embellishment.

For a rustic or north woods feel, use birch bark to make gift cards. Birch bark has a flexible, paperlike quality that lends itself well to this treatment. Use birch bark that has fallen from trees, or find sheets of it at floral or craft stores.

Cardboard is a handy, sturdy material that works well for making cards and tags. Or, cut windows in blank greeting cards, creating a frame to display your personal touches.

Framed greeting Card

MATERIALS

❖ Blank greeting card ❖ Photograph
❖ Transparent tape ❖ Art
paper ❖ Double-
sided tape

1 Cut a square, diamond, or other interesting shape in the front flap of card. Position photograph in opening as desired and secure with transparent tape on inside of front flap.

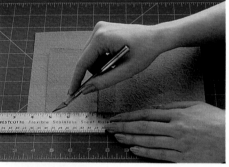

2 Cut art paper large enough to cover the taped back of photo-graph. Secure paper over photograph back with double-sided tape.

☞ *For quick construction, use ready-made blank framed greeting cards, such as art 'z' cards®; decorate as desired.*

☞ *For a card with a different twist, cut a piece of aluminum flashing to fit frame. Scratch flashing with 60-grit sandpaper, and secure to card with transparent tape. Further embellish card by securing buttons or floral materials to card with hot glue.*

Cardboard Card

MATERIALS

❖Heavy cardboard ❖Utility knife ❖Ruler ❖Nail ❖Raffia ❖Embellishments, such as photographs, buttons, twigs, and silk or dried flowers ❖Hot glue gun and glue sticks, or craft glue

1 Cut two pieces of cardboard to desired size, using utility knife. Place one piece on a flat surface. Use a ruler to cover a ¾" (2 cm) margin on the left side of the piece; bend the cardboard against the edge of the ruler a few times. (This bent piece will be the front part of your card.)

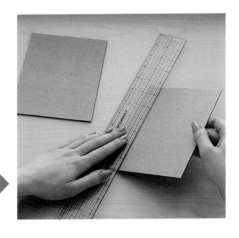

2 Make hole at top and bottom of left margin of bent piece, using a nail. Make matching holes in the second piece of cardboard. Thread two pieces of raffia through holes to secure cardboard pieces together; tie with a knot, and trim ends.

3 Secure desired embellishments to front of card, using hot glue or craft glue. Write message inside card.

☞ If the card is for someone going on a trip, embellish the front with a piece of map that shows their destination.

☞ For a more decorative writing space, secure a piece of art paper to the inside of the card, using hot glue or craft glue.

Tin Tag

MATERIALS

❖Foil pie plate or cake pan ❖Round, metal-rimmed hang tag ❖Hot glue gun and glue sticks, or craft glue

🎁

1 Cut out embossed design from the bottom of a pie plate or cake pan.

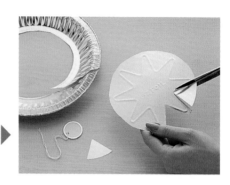

2 Write name or greeting on hang tag. Secure tag to center of tin tag, using hot glue or craft glue.

☞ *If desired, attach circle of art paper in place of hang tag to center of tin tag with hot glue; then punch a hole in tag with a nail. Thread decorative cord or raffia through hole, and tie off to make a loop.*

Shipping-tag Card

MATERIALS

❖Two shipping tags ❖Hot glue gun and glue sticks, or craft glue ❖Embellishments, such as dried floral materials ❖Raffia, ribbon, or cotton string

🎁

1 Join two shipping tags at the ends with the holes, using hot glue or craft glue. (The tags should open like a book.)

☞ *Use colored markers to draw a design on the front of the card.*

2 Embellish the top tag as desired. Write your message on the inside. Thread raffia, ribbon, or string through the hole in the card; tie to the gift.

☞ *In place of floral materials, secure torn pieces of colored art paper randomly to front of card with craft glue.*

Birch-bark Card

MATERIALS

❖Birch bark ❖Utility knife ❖Art paper
❖Hot glue gun and glue sticks

1 Cut birch bark to desired height and twice the desired width, using a utility knife. Bend the birch bark in half over the straight edge of a table to create a card.

2 Cut art paper so it is just smaller than the inside of the card. Attach paper to inside of bark card, using hot glue. Write message on paper.

☞ *If the edge of the card is rough, you may want to tear, instead of cut, the art paper, to match the edges.*

☞ *To make bark more pliable and easier to work with, soak it in warm water for several hours.*

PATINA-FINISHED Copper

Patina, the green film formed on copper after prolonged exposure to the elements, gives a unique, sophisticated look to gifts and cards. This verdigris finish can be easily duplicated using special antiquing solutions. You can cut the patina-finished copper into random designs and affix them to cards, using hot glue. Or make ornaments that can be used as gift tags or card decorations, then later reused to decorate a Christmas tree.

Copper sheets are readily available in craft stores, as are patina solutions. The sheets are easily cut with craft scissors, too.

Patina-finished Copper

MATERIALS

❖Copper sheet ❖Fine steel wool or 100-grit sandpaper ❖Antiquing solution for use on copper, such as Modern Options' Patina Green™ ❖Small glass or plastic bowls; applicators, such as stiff-bristled brush, sea sponge, or cloth rag ❖Matte finish aerosol clear acrylic sealer ❖Hot glue gun and glue sticks, or craft glue

1 Rub copper sheet with steel wool or sandpaper so it will better accept the verdigris solution; wipe clean.

2 Pour small amount of antiquing solution into bowl; apply solution to copper sheet, using desired applicator. Allow the solution to react with metal until dry.

3 Repeat step 2 until desired effect is achieved. Allow to dry. Apply two thin coats of aerosol acrylic sealer. Allow to dry.

4 Cut copper sheet into ornaments or abstract shapes, using craft scissors. Secure the pieces to cards or gifts, using hot glue or craft glue.

☞ *Secure ornament to book or card by punching holes in book cover, next to points of ornament, with awl. Thread thin wire through holes, and wrap around points of the ornament; twist ends of wire to secure.*

☞ *Use an awl or tin-punching tool to punch a hole in ornament or gift tag for a hanger.*

☞ *Write messages on prepared copper with permanent markers.*

☞ *Use prepared copper on Framed Greeting Cards (page 48).*

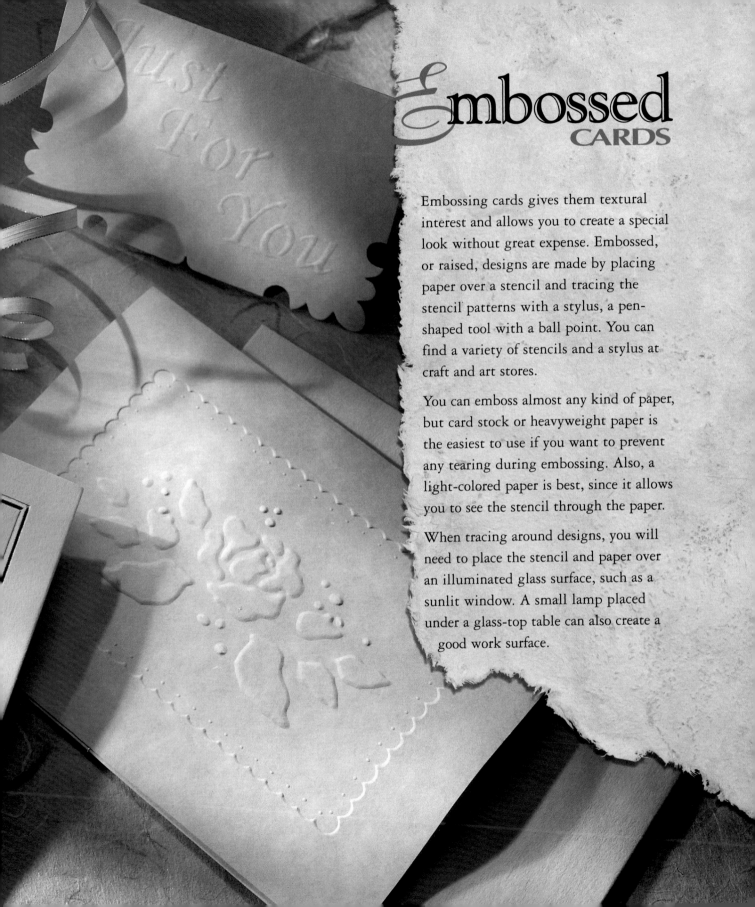

Embossed
CARDS

Embossing cards gives them textural interest and allows you to create a special look without great expense. Embossed, or raised, designs are made by placing paper over a stencil and tracing the stencil patterns with a stylus, a pen-shaped tool with a ball point. You can find a variety of stencils and a stylus at craft and art stores.

You can emboss almost any kind of paper, but card stock or heavyweight paper is the easiest to use if you want to prevent any tearing during embossing. Also, a light-colored paper is best, since it allows you to see the stencil through the paper.

When tracing around designs, you will need to place the stencil and paper over an illuminated glass surface, such as a sunlit window. A small lamp placed under a glass-top table can also create a good work surface.

Embossed Cards

MATERIALS

❖Card stock or heavyweight paper
❖Stencil with desired design ❖Stylus or
small plastic crochet hook
❖Removable transparent
tape ❖Illuminated
glass surface

1 Cut and fold paper to desired size for card. Position stencil as desired on front of card, and secure it with removable tape.

2 Place the card, stencil side down, on illuminated surface, such as a glass table with a lamp under it. Secure the card with removable tape.

3 Trace the outline of stencil design, applying firm pressure with a stylus. Retrace the design, if necessary, for clear definition. Trace around the outer edges of stencil to frame design, if desired.

☞ *If you are concerned that the removable tape may stick to card and tear it upon removal, press the tape a couple of times against your shirt or pants to make it less sticky; then use it to secure stencil.*

☞ *If stylus squeaks as you are tracing stencil design, lubricate the end by rubbing it in the palm of your hand.*

Edible TAGS

Edible gift tags are a delightful and delicious way to embellish a gift. These tags, which require only a little thought and effort on your part, can be created in a number of ways. They can even replace a traditional bow.

Remove the outer wrap from a flat candy bar, leaving the foil wrap in place. Rewrap the bar with plain colored paper to coordinate with your gift wrap. Write your greeting or the recipient's name on the newly wrapped bar, and attach to the gift with tape.

For a child's gift, cover a small box of candy with stickers. Attach the candy box to the gift with ribbon or hot glue. The child can keep the decorated box and reuse it after the candy is eaten.

Cookies and shapes cut from chocolate also make good tags. Prepared frosting is available in cans and squeeze tubes for easy decorating with little mess. To embellish your tags, choose from the many decorative candy toppings available in the baking goods aisle of your supermarket.

Chocolate Cutouts

MATERIALS

❖Baking sheet ❖Wax paper ❖12 oz. (340 g) imported sweet chocolate, broken in pieces ❖12 oz. (340 g) white baking chocolate, broken in pieces ❖Two microwaveproof bowls ❖Cookie cutters or sharp knife ❖Frosting in squeeze tube ❖Plastic wrap ❖Ribbon

1 Line the baking sheet with wax paper. Place sweet chocolate in microwave-proof bowl. Microwave at 50% (Medium) for 2 to 4 minutes, or until chocolate is glossy and can be stirred smooth, stirring twice.

2 Pour and spread the chocolate evenly on lined baking sheet. Place in freezer for 5 minutes, or until set.

3 Place white chocolate pieces in second bowl. Microwave at 50% (Medium) for 2 to 4 minutes, or until chocolate is glossy and can be stirred smooth, stirring twice. Cool slightly. Pour and spread evenly over sweet chocolate layer.

1 Cut licorice long enough to form a loop that can be attached to gift. Spread an even layer of frosting onto the back of one cookie.

2 Fold licorice in half to form a loop. Place cut ends of licorice in frosting on cookie. Place the back side of second cookie over the licorice and frosting; press gently. ▼

Sandwich cookie Tag

MATERIALS

❖Shoestring licorice ❖Two small cookies of desired shape ❖Frosting, in squeeze tubes or cans ❖Decorative candy toppings, such as cinnamon candies, confetti, colored shot, silver dragées, and sprinkles, if desired

3 Decorate one side of cookie tag with frosting and decorative candy toppings. Use squeeze-tube frosting to write recipient's name on tag.

4 Place layered chocolate in freezer for 5 minutes, or until set. Remove from freezer and let soften slightly. Cut desired shapes from chocolate with cookie cutters or sharp knife. Using squeeze-tube frosting, write names of recipients on shapes. Chill until set. ▶

5 Wrap each tag in a small piece of plastic wrap. Attach to gifts with ribbon.

☞ *If desired, sprinkle white chocolate layer with colored sugar or other decorative candy topping while chocolate is still wet.*

Recycled
BOXES

We all have leftover boxes that once held department store purchases, shoes, candy, and even cheese and sausages, kept "just in case." If the box is in good shape and isn't covered with writing, you may be able to skip the wrapping paper on your next gift and just embellish the box.

First, determine the theme you want to follow. For example, if your gift is a country cross-stitch sampler, you may want to trim the box with a gingham ribbon or dried florals, a vintage-style gift tag, and raffia. If the gift is more formal, like a crystal bowl or candlesticks, give the box an elegant look with gold or tapestry ribbon and trim.

Once you have your theme, look at the condition of your box. Take note of any scratches, dents, or printed logos. You'll want to cover these areas. If the logo is in the center of the box, focus on decorating from the center. If there is a dent on one corner of the lid, consider an asymmetrical design that covers only that area, or create balance by matching the embellishment on the opposite side or corner.

Tapestry Box

MATERIALS

❖Sturdy, dark-colored box ❖Wide tapestry ribbon ❖Narrow gold braid or ribbon ❖Hot glue gun and glue sticks, or craft glue

☞ *Box can be used to hold photographs or letters after gift is removed.*

1 Cut tapestry ribbon long enough to wrap around lid of box in desired direction plus 2" (5 cm). Secure ribbon to lid of box, using glue; fold 1" (2.5 cm) of each end under the edge of the lid, and secure with glue.

2 Cut two pieces of gold braid the same length as the tapestry ribbon; secure braid along each side of ribbon with glue.

Elegant bow Box

MATERIALS

❖Box with logo on center of lid ❖Gold wired ribbon ❖Hot glue gun and glue sticks

1 Cut two pieces of ribbon long enough to cross center of box and drape over sides. Apply a large dollop of hot glue to center of lid. Cross center of ribbons over glue; press to secure. (Place a piece of scrap paper over ribbons to avoid burning your fingers when pressing ribbons into place.)

2 Make cluster bow (page 34), using gold wired ribbon. Secure bow to top of box in center of crossed ribbons, using hot glue. Trim ends of ribbon as desired.

Dried floral *Box*

MATERIALS

❖Box with writing on side and top
❖Crinkled art paper ❖Hot glue gun and
glue sticks, or craft glue ❖Buttons or
other embellishments ❖Dried
floral materials with stems
❖Nail ❖Raffia

1 Cut piece of crinkled art paper in the desired shape, and large enough to cover writing on side of box; cut second piece large enough to cover writing on top of box. Secure pieces of paper to side and top of box, using hot glue or craft glue.

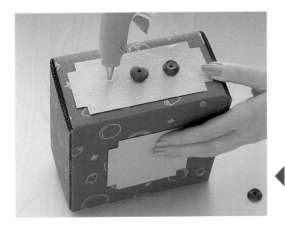

2 Glue buttons to side of box covered with paper. Use this side as front of box.

3 Place bundle of dried floral materials on top of box with stems pointing toward front of box. Using nail, punch holes in top of box on both sides of stems. Thread raffia through the holes from inside of box; tie bundled floral materials securely in place.

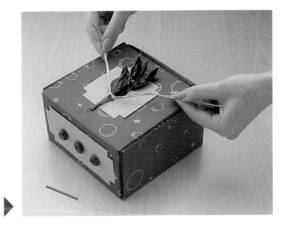

67

EASY
Painted boxes

You don't have to be that artistic or even have a lot of extra time to give a plain gift box a stylish look. Light-colored or white boxes with textured surfaces and little or no printing work best for the simple painting techniques shown at left.

Antiqued Box

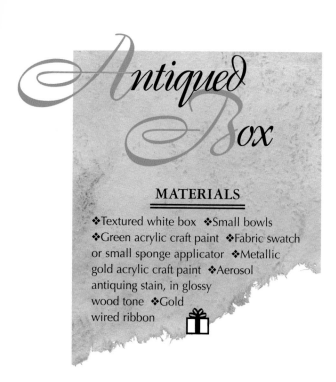

MATERIALS

❖Textured white box ❖Small bowls
❖Green acrylic craft paint ❖Fabric swatch
or small sponge applicator ❖Metallic
gold acrylic craft paint ❖Aerosol
antiquing stain, in glossy
wood tone ❖Gold
wired ribbon

1 Remove lid from box; set aside. Pour a small amount of green paint into bowl. Paint all four sides and bottom of box base with green paint, using sponge applicator. Allow to dry.

2 Pour a small amount of gold paint into second bowl. Dip fabric swatch or sponge into gold paint. Dab paint over entire outside surface of lid. (Paint does not have to be even but should cover entire surface.) Allow to dry.

Framed-painting Box

MATERIALS

❖Sturdy box with semishiny surface
❖Painter's tape ❖Two coordinating colors
of acrylic craft paint ❖Small bowls ❖Two
small, natural-bristle paintbrushes ❖Heavy
gold cording ❖Hot glue gun
and glue sticks ❖Small
scrap of leather
or art paper

1 Apply painter's tape to top center of box lid, creating a square or rectangle; press inner edges of tape firmly in place.

2 Pour a small amount of each color of paint into two separate bowls. Dip paintbrush into one color. Starting on tape on lower half of taped-off area, stroke the paintbrush in a wavy pattern over entire lower half.

☞ *If more color is desired, spray entire box with aerosol acrylic paint prior to decorating. Allow to dry.*

☞ *The semishiny surface of the box prevents tape from peeling surface of box upon removal.*

3 Spray both sections of box with antiquing stain until desired level of antiquing is achieved. Allow to dry.

4 Place gift in box. Tie ribbon around box; make bow.

Leaf-patterned Box

MATERIALS

❖Textured white box ❖Aerosol acrylic paint in green and gold
❖Dried pressed leaf
❖Aerosol adhesive

1 Spray lid of box with green paint; allow to dry.

2 Apply aerosol adhesive lightly to the back of pressed leaf; wait 15 to 30 seconds. Press leaf in place on lid of box.

3 Spray lid and bottom of box with gold paint; allow to dry. Remove leaf.

3 Dip the second paintbrush in second bowl of paint. Apply paint in same manner as before in top half of taped-off area. Blend two colors slightly by brushing into area with first color while paint is still wet. If desired, blend paint through entire area. Allow to dry.

4 Remove tape. Cut cording long enough to frame the painted area. Secure cording around edge of painted area, using hot glue. Place a drop of hot glue at point where ends of cording meet. Press small piece of leather or art paper over glue to conceal ends.

Creative
GIFT BAGS

Paper bags are a simple and versatile way to present your gifts. They come in a variety of sizes and are perfect for odd-shaped and hard-to-wrap items.

Paper bags are available in solid colors or printed patterns. There are several easy ways to put creative personal touches on the gift bag of your choice. Attach ornaments or small toys to the handles of bags with curling ribbon, allowing the long, curly ends to hang down the side of the bag. Attach tags or cards to the handles with ribbon, raffia, or cording, depending on the look you want.

Tissue paper is a key element of gift-bag presentation. It is available in a wide variety of colors, and some styles have prints or patterns on them. Layer several colors of tissue in the bag, one sheet at a time; then fluff the edges to conceal the object in the bag. For a bag with an Egyptian pattern, such as the one shown at left, use beige, burgundy, and gold-colored tissues. Tissue printed with a map pattern could add to the global look of the bag.

If you have several small gifts, place them in assorted individual bags filled with a variety of tissue colors. Place the small bags in a larger bag with more tissue.

Friendship
BAGS

Basic gift bags are an easy way to "wrap" gifts. For fun, you can customize bags for recipients by decorating them with mementos, pictures, and designs.

If the gift is going to a close friend, attach items that depict memorable times you've had, such as cut-out photographs, key words cut from magazines, theater ticket stubs, the label from a shared bottle of champagne, or even subway tokens. For someone who is going on a trip, a "Bon Voyage" gift can be placed in a bag decorated with maps, post cards, the wrapper from an imported candy bar, and foreign currency.

Gift bags can also be tailored to an event, such as Christmas or a birthday. Embellish the bag with images made from construction paper, flowers, pictures, sequins, buttons, or beads. You may even want to start a revolving gift bag which you and a friend trade back and forth, adding embellishments from year to year.

Attach paper items to bags with double-sided tape or paper cement. Ordinary craft glue causes the paper to buckle. Attach heavier items, such as buttons or coins, with hot glue. Use colored tissue paper to fill the bag around the gift, and fluff the tissue at the top to conceal the gift.

Embellished
BASKETS

Simple, inexpensive baskets can be made to look extraordinary with basic materials and a little of your time. Tailor-make a basket that will be on display long after the gift has been removed.

For a homespun look, the embellishments can be as simple as torn fabric strips tied in simple bows around a basket. Or you may want to secure dried flowers to the basket. To achieve an elegant look for the holidays, decorate a basket with pinecones and paint it metallic gold. Whatever style you choose, the techniques are simple.

Eucalyptus Basket

MATERIALS

❖Light-colored basket with handle
❖Preserved eucalyptus branches ❖Dried
red yarrow ❖22-gauge or 24-gauge
paddle floral wire and
wire cutter
❖Raffia 🎁

1 Cut several 3" to 4" (7.5 to 10 cm) stems of eucalyptus and yarrow. Set aside.

2 Cut paddle wire into two or more 30" (76 cm) lengths, depending on the size of your basket. Thread end of wire through the lip of the basket next to handle, and twist tightly to secure end. ▶

Gold pinecone Basket

MATERIALS

❖Loosely woven wire or grapevine basket
❖Pinecones ❖22-gauge or 24-gauge
paddle floral wire and wire cutter
❖Metallic gold aerosol
paint ❖Glitter,
optional 🎁

1 Secure pinecones to basket, using paddle floral wire, as in steps 2 and 3, above.

2 Place basket on newspaper in well-ventilated area. Apply one or two coats of gold aerosol paint. If desired, sprinkle pinecones lightly with glitter while paint is still wet.

☞ *For a rustic-style basket, cover entire basket with small pinecones, and leave pinecones unpainted.*

3 Position a few pieces of eucalyptus and one piece of yarrow along lip of basket, next to end of wire. Secure pieces to basket by threading wire through basket weave and looping around stems. Continue to add pieces of eucalyptus and yarrow and secure in this manner. When you reach end of wire, secure to a second piece of wire by twisting ends together.

4 Tie raffia in bow around handle of basket to embellish.

☞ *This technique could also be used with dried baby's breath in the spring or bittersweet in the fall.*

1 Tear strips from fabric that are about 2" (5 cm) wide and 24" (61 cm) long. (Length may vary depending on the size of the basket.)

Country fabric bow Basket

MATERIALS

❖Basket without handle ❖Assorted coordinating quilt fabrics
❖Large-eyed needle

2 Thread a fabric strip through eye of needle. Insert needle through weave of basket near top. Tie bow; allow ends to hang down. Trim ends of bow as desired. Repeat for additional bows.

Shrink-wrapped GIFTS

Filled gift baskets and containers are classic gifts, but purchasing prepared baskets can be expensive, and you may not get exactly what you want in them. Creating personalized, shrink-wrapped gifts takes only a little extra effort, and your recipient will know that you put some special thought into the gift. Shrink wrap is available at most craft stores and will add a finished professional touch to your gift.

Start by selecting the gift items; then choose a container of correct size to hold everything. You can use baskets, buckets, decorative tins, or even large cups or mugs. Fillers, like excelsior, a shredded wood product available at craft stores; dried naturals, like pinecones, flowers, and nuts; crumpled tissue paper; or even wrapped candies will help lift and secure items in the container. When your items are satisfactorily arranged, you can shrink-wrap the entire container to ensure that everything will stay in place.

Packing & shrink-wrapping Baskets

MATERIALS

❖Basket ❖Multiple gifts to be placed in basket ❖Filler material, such as excelsior or tissue ❖Bow or other embellishment, optional ❖Shrink wrap ❖Transparent tape ❖Hair dryer

☞ *Use shrinkable window plastic, cut to size, for large baskets.*

☞ *For Christmas, you could fill large holiday mugs with a prepared mix for a holiday drink, like Tom & Jerries or mulled cider, and a bag of special holiday cookies.*

☞ *A "pamper yourself" basket may include a bottle of wine, a book, bubble bath, a loofa or back brush, and a compact disk or tape with relaxing music.*

1 Arrange gifts in basket, using filler to lift smaller items above the edge of the basket. Pack filler around large, heavy items to keep them from shifting in basket. Strive to achieve a look that is visually appealing. ▼

2 Attach a bow or other embellishment to handle of basket or to an item in basket, if desired. Take into consideration that items secured to the outside of the handle may be pressed flat by the shrink-wrapping process.

3 Open shrink wrap and place over basket, laying folded edge of wrap on top of basket. Carefully, gather and tuck extra wrap under the bottom of basket and secure with tape. Cut away any excess wrap.

4 Shrink the wrap by directing air from the hair dryer toward the bottom of basket. Direct the air around bottom of basket, working up to edge of basket.

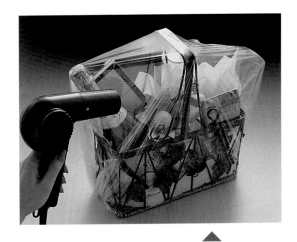

5 Direct air from hair dryer along basket handle until wrap shrinks tightly to handle. Use a back-and-forth motion to shrink the remaining loose wrap to the rest of the basket.

CLAY POTS *as* Containers

Terra-cotta pots and saucers are good for more than just plants. They can be uniquely decorated for gift containers, and the container becomes an additional gift. This concept provides you with a clever packaging idea with minimal expense, effort, and waste. Choose from among terra-cotta pots, plastic pots, and the myriad decorated pots on the market.

Inverting one saucer over another provides you with a simple, sturdy package that will protect small, fragile gifts. It can double as a garlic roaster, too.

A delightful honey pot is a gift all by itself. Just paint a pot yellow, cover it with an inverted saucer, and fill it up with "a little something," like jars of flavored honey, honey soap, honey candies, or tea bags and honey straws.

Buttons, stones, glass beads, or small charms can be used to embellish a terra-cotta pot. Use your imagination to come up with a decorating scheme.

Saucer Packaging

MATERIALS

❖Two terra-cotta pot saucers in desired size ❖Heavy craft paper ❖Craft glue ❖Ribbon ❖Raffia

🎁

1 Place gift in one saucer. Invert second saucer over gift. Wrap a wide strip of heavy paper around saucers and secure overlapped ends with craft glue. Glue a slightly narrower strip of ribbon over the paper. Tie raffia over the ribbon to complete the look.

☞ *Two unpainted, unglazed 6" (15 cm) terra-cotta saucers can be used as a garlic roaster after the gift inside is removed. Include the instructions at right with the gift.*

☞ *For a holiday version, paint the saucers with gold paint and tie with a festive ribbon.*

Soak saucers in clean, warm water for 15 minutes. Cut the tops off whole garlic heads so each garlic clove is exposed. If desired, drizzle olive oil over exposed cloves. Place garlic heads in one saucer and cover with second saucer. Place in a cold oven. Turn oven on to 350°F and roast for 1 to 1½ hours, or until garlic is very soft. Squeeze roasted garlic paste out of slightly cooled garlic head. Use as a spread on toasted Italian bread.

Honey Pot

MATERIALS

❖Terra-cotta pot and saucer with equal diameters ❖Gold or yellow acrylic paint ❖Foam brush ❖Black permanent-ink marker ❖Hot glue gun and glue sticks ❖Silk flowers or other embellishments ❖Sisal rope ❖Raffia

🎁

1 Apply two coats gold or yellow acrylic paint over entire pot and saucer, using a foam brush. Allow paint to dry between coats.

2 Write the word "honey" in an arch on one side of the pot, using black marker. Secure flowers or other embellishments to pot, using hot glue.

1 Secure embellishments to outside of pot, using craft glue. Space embellishments randomly on pot. ▼

2 Layer several pieces of tissue paper on one another. Place gift in center. Gather tissue around top of gift and place in pot. Fluff tissue to conceal gift.

Jeweled Pot

MATERIALS

❖Terra-cotta pot ❖Embellishments, such as imitation jewels, beads, or buttons ❖Craft glue ❖Colored tissue paper

☞ *For a more colorful package, apply at least two layers of acrylic paint to pot and allow to dry before attaching embellishments. Or purchase prepainted or glazed pots.*

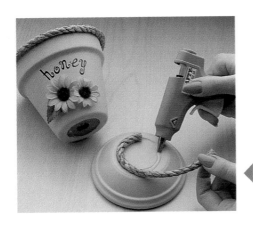

3 Cut piece of sisal rope to fit around the top rim of the pot; secure to rim with hot glue. Cut second piece to form embellishment on the center of saucer bottom; secure to saucer with hot glue.

4 Invert saucer onto the pot after filling pot. Secure saucer to pot with raffia tied at the top.

idea

WRAPPING SMALL
Specialty items

Specialty soaps, lotions, and perfumes are popular, inexpensive gifts that can be enhanced with simple wrapping and presentation ideas.

For an assortment of toiletries, wrap both the lid and bottom of a gift box with floral wrapping paper. Decorate the lid with silk ribbons. Fill the tissue-lined box with washcloths, soap, bath gel, talcum powder, and other small items.

Individual specialty soaps can be partially wrapped with decorative papers or fabrics and embellished with dried floral materials. Arrange an assortment of these wrapped soaps in a basket or bowl lined with potpourri or sprigs of preserved evergreen.

Transfer liquid soap, lotion, or bath oil to a small, decorative bottle. Wrap the bottle neck with a pretty ribbon and add a wax seal with the recipient's initial, following manufacturer's directions. You can place the bottle in a gift box or present it as is.

Creative
GIFT PACKING

Thoughtful gift presentations shouldn't stop with the outside of the gift box. Create visual excitement when the box is opened by using decorative tissues, ribbons, and other items to pack around your gift. These fillers protect your gift as well as highlight it and are especially nice when gifts are shipped in plain brown boxes.

Fill the space around children's gifts with wrapped hard candies. Use table tennis balls or pinecones in large gift boxes. A gift for someone at the office can be surrounded by shredded printer paper. Excelsior, Mylar® foil, wrapping paper, or any other loose, bulky item can be used as a filler.

A multitude of colored and patterned tissue paper can be crumpled, cut into strips, or used to loosely wrap the gift within the box. For formal gifts, use patterned white or cream tissue with gold accents.

☞ *For a simple, elegant look, use gold tissue, or patterned cream or white tissue paper to line a gift box.*

☞ *If wrapping a wedding gift, try to match the tissue or filler to the bride's colors.*

Tissue Streamers

MATERIALS

❖ Folded tissue paper   ❖ Pinking shears

1 Make streamers by cutting the folded tissue with pinking shears to desired width. Fluff the streamers and fill space around gift. Use more than one color of tissue, if desired. ▼

Rainbow Tissue

MATERIALS

❖ Assorted colored tissue papers

1 Place gift in center of the box. Individually crumple and twist a variety of brightly colored tissues into loose balls or rosettes. Pack the crumpled tissue around gift inside the box.

1 Cut pieces of tissue and cellophane large enough to wrap around gift and have several extra inches on sides. Place tissue over cellophane so the edges match.

2 Roll tissue and cellophane around the gift. Gather sides together, and tie with ribbon. Place "candy" in center of gift box and surround with wrapped candies. ▼

Candy Filler

MATERIALS

❖Tissue ❖Transparent colored cellophane
❖Ribbon ❖Wrapped candies

INDEX

CREDITS

CY DECOSSE INCORPORATED

Chairman/CEO: Bruce Barnet
Chairman Emeritus: Cy DeCosse
President/COO: Nino Tarantino
Executive V.P./Editor-in-Chief:
  William B. Jones

WRAP IT UP
Created by: The Editors of
  Cy DeCosse Incorporated

Also available from the publisher:
Grand Slam Gifts, Greet the Season,
Toast the Host

Group Executive Editor: Zoe A. Graul
Editorial Manager: Dawn M. Anderson
Senior Editor/Writer: Ellen C. Boeke
Project Manager: Amy Berndt
Associate Creative Director: Lisa Rosenthal
Art Director: Stephanie Michaud
Editor: Janice Cauley

Researcher/Designer: Michael Basler
Sample Production Manager: Carol Olson
Technical Photo Stylists: Bridget Haugh,
  Sue Jorgensen, Abigail Wyckoff
Styling Director: Bobbette Destiche
Project Stylists: Christine Jahns,
  Joanne Wawra
Prop Stylist: Michele Joy
Food Stylist: Nancy Johnson
Artisans: Arlene Dohrman,
  Phyllis Galbraith, Kristi Kuhnau,
  Virginia Mateen, Carol Pilot,
  Michelle Skudlarek
Vice President of Development Planning &
  Production: Jim Bindas
Director of Photography: Mike Parker
Creative Photo Coordinator:
  Cathleen Shannon
Studio Manager: Marcia Chambers
Lead Photographer: Mike Parker
Photographers: Rex Irmen, Charles Nields,
  Rebecca Schmitt
Contributing Photographers: Paul Najlis,
  Steve Smith
Print Production Manager: Patt Sizer
Desktop Publishing Specialist:
  Laurie Kristensen
Production Staff: Tom Heck,
  Laura Hokkanen, Tom Hoops,
  Jeanette Moss, Michelle Peterson,
  Mike Schauer, Michael Sipe,
  Greg Wallace, Kay Wethern

Shop Supervisor: Phil Juntti
Scenic Carpenters: Troy Johnson,
  Rob Johnstone, John Nadeau
Contributors: art 'z' cards; Design Master;
  Duff Associates; Forestsaver; Loose Ends;
  Modern Options; Plaid Enterprises;
  The Reynolds Wrap Kitchens
Sources for Product Information:
  Framed greeting cards—art 'z' cards,
  P.O. Box 6568, Bozeman, MT 59771,
  (800) 789-6503

  Copper verdigris solution/Patina Green—
  MODERN OPTIONS, 2325 3rd Street,
  #339, San Francisco, CA 94107,
  (415) 252-5580

  Colored plastic wrap—Reynolds Metals
  Co. Consumer Response Dept.,
  (800) 433-2244
Printed on American paper by:
  R. R. Donnelley & Sons Co. (0796)
99 98 97 96 / 5 4 3 2 1

Cy DeCosse Incorporated offers
a variety of how-to books. For
information write:
  Cy DeCosse Subscriber Books
  5900 Green Oak Drive
  Minnetonka, MN 55343